SPOTLIGHT ON THE CIVIL RIGHTS MOVEMENT™

THE LITTLE ROCK DESEGREGATION CRISIS

MARCIA AMIDON LÜSTED

Rosen
YA™
New York

Published in 2018 by The Rosen Publishing Group, Inc.
29 East 21st Street, New York, NY 10010

Library of Congress Cataloging-in-Publication Data

Names: Lüsted, Marcia Amidon, author.
Title: The Little Rock desegregation crisis / Marcia Amidon Lusted.
Description: New York : Rosen Publishing, 2018. | Series: Spotlight on the civil rights movement | Includes bibliographical references and index. | Audience: Grades 5–10.
Identifiers: LCCN 2017019696| ISBN 9781538380444 (library bound) | ISBN 9781538380413 (pbk.) | ISBN 9781538380420 (6 pack)
Subjects: LCSH: School integration—Arkansas—Little Rock—Juvenile literature. | Discrimination in educa-tion—Arkansas—Little Rock—Juvenile literature. | African Americans—Education—Arkansas—Little Rock—Juvenile literature. | African American students—Arkansas—Little Rock—Juvenile literature. | Little Rock (Ark.)—Race relations—Juvenile literature. | Central High School (Little Rock, Ark.)—Juvenile literature.
Classification: LCC LA242.L5 L87 2018 | DDC 379.2/630976773—dc23
LC record available at https://lccn.loc.gov/2017019696

Manufactured in China

On the cover: National Guard soldiers escort black students into the newly desegregated Little Rock High School after an influential court ruling changed the composition of classrooms once and for all.

CONTENTS

SEPTEMBER 4, 1957

It was the second day of school at Central High School in Little Rock, Arkansas. It was supposed to be the beginning of a new era for Little Rock schools. For the first time, black students would be allowed to attend a white high school.

Two hundred and fifty members of the Arkansas National Guard surrounded the school. The governor, Orval Faubus, had ordered them there. He claimed he had sent the National Guard to protect citizens. But then Elizabeth Eckford, a black student, tried to enter Central High. She recalled:

> I walked up to the guard who had let [several white students] in. When I tried to squeeze past him, he raised his bayonet, and then the other guards moved in and raised their bayonets ... Somebody started yelling, "Lynch her! Lynch her!

Federal troops stand guard in front of Central High School in Little Rock, Arkansas, to enforce desegregation laws.

Segregation, where black and white students attended separate schools, was supposed to be over. But in Little Rock, that would not happen without a fight.

BROWN v. BOARD OF EDUCATION

I n 1954, the United States Supreme Court ruled that segregating children in public schools was a violation of the Fourteenth Amendment to the Constitution. The court stated that the practice of having "separate but equal" schools for black and white students was unconstitutional. This ruling was the result of a court case, *Brown v. Board of Education*. This case was filed in Topeka, Kansas, by a parent who claimed that his black child had been denied access to a white school. He contended that the segregated schools there were not and would never be equal. The court agreed that education "is a right which must be made available to all on equal terms."

William Gordon (*right*), managing editor of the African American newspaper *Atlantic Daily World*, reads a headline about the Supreme Court's decision to end school segregation.

The case became a legal means for challenging segregation in schools all over the United States. It inspired school reforms and active enforcement of other civil rights laws as well. *Brown v. Board of Education* helped spark the civil rights movement.

LITTLE ROCK, ARKANSAS

ittle Rock was a test of the desegregation process. Southern states were very slow to begin desegregation, even though the Supreme Court outlawed it in 1954. Little Rock's school board had been one of the first to issue a statement after *Brown v. Board of Education.* They said, "It is our responsibility to comply with federal constitutional requirements, and we intend to do so when the Supreme Court … outlines the methods to be followed." Little Rock was already known for its progressive attitude about desegregation. Its university had admitted black students since 1948. Thirty-three percent of all eligible blacks in Arkansas were registered to vote. Blacks had joined the police force. Libraries, parks, and public buses were integrated. Many blacks and whites lived next door to each other in integrated neighborhoods. Daisy Bates, head of the Arkansas National Association for the Advancement of Colored People (NAACP), called Little Rock "a liberal southern city."

Daisy Bates, a civil rights leader and an official of the NAACP, stands outside her office during the Little Rock crisis.

THE BLOSSOM PLAN

Because of Little Rock's relatively liberal policies, it seemed like a good place to test desegregation. So, in 1954, it was time to make a plan for integrating its schools.

Little Rock's superintendent of schools, Virgil T. Blossom, created a plan to desegregate the schools during the summer of 1954. The community had two new high schools under construction. It seemed logical to start integration with them when they opened in the fall of 1956.

On May 24, 1955, the school board voted to adopt a watered-down version of Blossom's plan. Only one high school, Central High, would be integrated, and not until the fall of 1957. Other schools would follow even more slowly. Only a few black students would be allowed to join the two thousand white students attending Central. The board wanted to move cautiously. Despite the board's caution, both whites and blacks opposed this version of the plan.

School superintendent Virgil T. Blossom created the plan to desegregate Little Rock schools in 1954.

SEGREGATIONIST SUMMER

The summer of 1957 was a time of public dissatisfaction with desegregation. As the first day of school came closer, the school board tried to quietly reduce the number of black students who would attend Central High. They required any black student who wanted to go there to register and pass a screening process. Only twenty-five students made it through the screenings, and the school board tried to convince them not to attend.

By September, only nine students were enrolled at Central. NAACP lawyer Wiley Branton said, "The nine of the twenty-five [were] selected by the school board because they were trying to get 'good' Negroes, and none of the 'radicals.'" The "radicals"

Photographed here are seven of the Little Rock Nine students (*from left*): Carlotta Walls, Gloria Ray, Ernest Green, Jefferson Thomas, Thelma Mothershed, Terrance Roberts, and Minnijean Brown. Jane Hill (*far right*) is not considered part of the Little Rock Nine because her parents did not allow her to participate after the first day.

were the children of parents who had sued the school board because desegregation was taking too long.

These nine students would later become known as the Little Rock Nine. They would earn themselves a place in the history books.

THE LITTLE ROCK NINE

The Little Rock Nine students were Minnijean Brown, Elizabeth Eckford, Ernest Green, Thelma Mothershed, Melba Patillo, Gloria Ray, Terrence Roberts, Jefferson Thomas, and Carlotta Walls. Each ranged from fifteen to eighteen years old. They had been recruited and carefully screened by Daisy Bates and her husband, L. C. Bates. Bates and her husband published an influential African American newspaper, the *Arkansas State Press*. With help from other NAACP members, Bates decided that these nine students had the determination and strength to face what would most likely be a tough situation. Many people in Little Rock were strongly against integration. The Little Rock Nine would have to walk into a potentially violent situation. Before school started, they attended counseling sessions about what to expect and how to handle hostile situations.

Would they be ready?

Jane Hill (*left*) and Elizabeth Eckford were two of the students who attempted to attend Little Rock Central High School on the first day of classes.

THE MOTHERS' LEAGUE

A new group of whites formed at the end of the summer. They called themselves the Mothers' League, and they were against desegregation. At the urging of Governor Faubus, they filed a temporary injunction, which is a legal order to prevent an action. They wanted Central High to be for white students only. The head of the group, Mrs. Clyde A. Thomason, argued that both black and white students were buying knives and guns because they expected violence during the first day of school. Parents were afraid to send their children to Central High. The injunction was granted in court, delaying desegregation indefinitely.

Governor Orval Faubus of Arkansas poses with members of the Mothers' League. The women had marched to the governor's mansion to ask him to close Central High School rather than desegregate it.

A few days later, NAACP attorneys Wiley Branton and Thurgood Marshall asked a federal court to overturn the injunction. The judge ruled that there was no concrete evidence that violence would happen and ruled that desegregation would proceed.

MOVING AHEAD

Schools were supposed to open in Little Rock on September 3, 1957. The day before, Governor Faubus went on television and announced that he was going to surround Central High School with soldiers from the national guard.

He insisted, "[The soldiers] will not act as segregationists or integrationists but as soldiers …" Because of the violence Faubus expected to occur, the soldiers would actually be keeping black students out of Central High. Faubus had decided that because of what he saw as inevitable violence, the schools must still be operated on a segregated basis. Even though *Brown v. Board of Education* had been decided three years earlier, and it ordered desegregation to proceed "with all deliberate speed," Faubus ignored the ruling. He said, "Blood will run in the streets, if Negro pupils should attempt to enter Central High School." His words shocked not only Little Rock, but the entire United States.

Two young children watch as members of the National Guard patrol near Central High School.

CALLING IN THE GUARD

The Capital Citizens' Council (CCC) was an organization founded to resist the nation's school desegregation efforts. Made up of about five hundred members, it became the most important organization involved in the Little Rock desegregation crisis. It also sponsored the creation of the Mothers' League, which held a sunrise church service on September 3, 1957.

Angry parents of white students, the CCC, and local religious leaders all attended. They praised Governor Faubus, sang the song "Dixie," and raised a Confederate flag. This protest did not change the mind of Judge Ronald Davies, who had ruled that black students would attend Central the next day, September 4.

Soldiers from the Arkansas National Guard arrived in Little Rock. Faubus made the claim that the guard's arrival would protect the lives of the Little Rock Nine, not just keep them out of school.

The guard stood on the sidewalks outside Central High, surrounding it and forming a silent wall.

A woman and a boy hold protest signs during a march on the Arkansas capitol.

FIRST DAY OF SCHOOL

Daisy Bates worried that if the parents of the nine black students took them to school, they could incite a riot. She decided that she would accompany all of the students and they would arrive as a group. She sent messages to the nine to meet her at 8:30 a.m., and two police cars would drive them to school.

Everyone received Bates's message except for Elizabeth Eckford. Her parents did not have a telephone. As she got ready for school that morning, she could see that her parents were upset. She told them not to worry, then she left to catch the school bus. She wore a brand-new dress that she and her mother had made just for this day. Elizabeth rode off alone, to face her first day at Central High School.

These three rifles belonged to members of the National Guard. The Guard was ordered to the school by Governor Faubus, to prevent African American students from entering.

ELIZABETH ECKFORD

When Elizabeth stepped off the bus, she saw a huge crowd of white people and hundreds of soldiers with guns, all around the high school. One of the most famous photographs of this day shows Elizabeth walking into school, followed by a group of people shouting, their faces twisted with hate. The look on her face is one of calm and determination. This photograph of Elizabeth and the hostile crowd around her was printed and reprinted in newspapers across the country and internationally.

Still, she continued on. She tried to enter the school, but the soldiers turned her away. Elizabeth looked for a friendly face in the mob. "I looked into the face of an old woman and it seemed like a kind face, but when I looked at her again, she spat on me," Elizabeth later said.

In what is probably the most famous image from Little Rock, Elizabeth Eckford endures the screams of an angry mob as she walks to Central High.

Members of the Arkansas National Guard stop Elizabeth Eckford from entering Little Rock's Central High School.

The chant of the mob of men, women, and teenagers rang in Elizabeth's ears. "Two, four, six, eight, we ain't gonna integrate."

She ran for a bench at the bus stop, only wanting to go home, but the mob followed her, jeering. Then Benjamin Fine, a writer for the *New York Times*, put his arm around her. "He raised my chin and said, 'Don't let them see you cry,'" she said. A white woman named Grace Lorch, whose husband taught at a black college, led her away from the mob. Together they got on a bus, and Lorch helped Elizabeth get home safely.

The other eight students arrived at Central with Daisy Bates. They were turned away by soldiers as well, but they did not have to face the mob alone as Elizabeth Eckford had.

The next day Judge Davies asked the US Justice Department to investigate Governor Faubus's disruption of the integration plan.

The Alabama National Guard soldiers remained at Central High School, and the nine students remained at home. Governor Faubus went on TV to say that he still opposed desegregation. The Little Rock school board tried again to have the federal court suspend the desegregation plan, but the court refused again. Judge Davies's investigation resulted in legal action against the governor and several guardsmen for interfering with integration. Faubus still refused to remove the soldiers from Central High. The nine students were still not allowed to go to school.

Civil rights leader Martin Luther King Jr. took special notice of the events in Little Rock. He sent a telegram to President Eisenhower that urged the president to act. He said that unless the federal government got involved, the cause of integration would be set back fifty years. Eisenhower knew that the situation was becoming a conflict between state and federal governments. Soon he would be forced to take action.

Little Rock Nine student Ernest Green (*left*) shakes hands with Daisy Bates.
Civil rights leader Reverend Martin Luther King Jr. stands with them.

Faubus had defied federal court orders and prevented the integration of Central High School. But he was also nervous about how President Eisenhower might respond. He even sent Eisenhower a telegram, asking him to modify the desegregation rulings of the federal courts.

On September 14, Faubus met with President Eisenhower. Eisenhower said that the Alabama National Guard should only have been placed at Central High School to protect the black students. They should not have been scaring them away at gunpoint.

Faubus listened to the president's comments. But then he suggested that Eisenhower also defy the federal courts and order a

President Dwight D. Eisenhower and Governor Orval Faubus of Arkansas shake hands following a conference in Washington, DC, on September 14, 1957.

one-year delay in desegregating Little Rock. Eisenhower refused. On September 20, Faubus was ordered to remove the state national guard soldiers.

He did at last.

SEPTEMBER 23

Finally, on September 23, 1957, the nine students were going to school. They rode in two cars. When they arrived at Central High, they were escorted into a side entrance by police officers. An angry crowd of a thousand people milled around outside. Several reporters were attacked. Melba Patillo, one of the Little Rock Nine, later said, "I had long dreamed of entering Central High. I could not have imagined what that privilege could cost me."

Some white students jumped out of the school windows to avoid the black students. Others treated them fairly. But as the mob outside the building grew larger and more violent, Little Rock's chief of police decided that the safest thing to do would

A protestor, his face bloody, is led away by police after he and thousands of other people attempted to break through police lines outside Central High.

be to send the black students home. "The police were having difficulty holding back the mob at the barricade, and they said if they broke through they could not be responsible for our safety," student Ernest Green recalled.

TRYING AGAIN

The Little Rock Nine went home. Finally, on September 25, President Eisenhower ordered federal troops to Little Rock to protect the black students. The nine were escorted into Central High by these soldiers. Each one was also assigned a soldier as a bodyguard. Daisy Bates commented, "Any time it takes eleven thousand five hundred soldiers to assure nine Negro children their constitutional rights in a democratic society, I can't be happy."

Meanwhile, General Edwin Walker of the US Army addressed all of Central High's white students in the auditorium. "You have nothing to fear from my soldiers, and no one will interfere with your coming, going, or your peaceful pursuit of your studies," he said.

Troops escorted African American students in and out of Central High after desegregation took place.

Once the black students arrived, the white students had mixed reactions. One of them commented that "if parents would just go home and let us alone, we'll be all right ... we just want them to leave us be. We can do it."

OCCUPIED TERRITORY

Governor Faubus continued to fight against desegregation. He protested against the presence of federal troops. He said, "We are now in occupied territory. Evidence of the naked force of the federal government is here apparent, in these, unsheathed bayonets in the backs of schoolgirls." He insisted that the situation could have been resolved peacefully if he'd been given more time. But his tactics had also lost him political support.

By the last day of September, most of the federal troops had returned to their base, twelve miles (nineteen kilometers) away. But school life was not easy for the nine black students. They were bullied and harassed. Elizabeth Eckford wanted to leave but the vice principal persuaded her to stay. Minnijean

Governor Faubus holds up a national newspaper with a headline about forced desegregation during a press conference on September 28, 1957.

Brown was suspended when she lost her temper and dumped a bowl of chili on the head of a white boy who was taunting her. Later a card circulated among segregationist students, reading, "One down … eight to go."

CLOSING THE SCHOOLS

On May 28, 1958, Ernest Green became the first black student to graduate from Central High. Federal troops stood guard. Martin Luther King Jr. attended, almost unnoticed. When Green's name was announced, no one clapped. But Green said, "After I got that diploma, that was it. I had accomplished what I had come there for."

In July, Governor Faubus won a third term as governor. He was not finished opposing desegregation, which he referred to as "forced integration." In September 1958, he cited new state laws as a reason to close all four of Little Rock's high schools. They remained closed for the entire school year until a federal court ordered them reopened. More than 3,500 students of Little Rock were denied an education in what would later become known as the Lost Year.

Ernest Green, who became the first African American to graduate from Central High, puts on his cap and gown before the ceremony.

AFTERWORD

Governor Orval Faubus would go on to serve six consecutive terms as Alabama's governor. Little Rock's high schools finally reopened in August 1959.

Of the nine black students who attended Central High, Carlotta Walls and Jefferson Thomas returned to graduate in 1960. The rest finished high school at other schools or by correspondence courses. Several of the students went on to have distinguished careers. Ernest Green worked in President Jimmy Carter's administration. Minnijean Brown worked for President Bill Clinton's administration. Melba Patillo became a reporter for NBC.

In 1999, all of the Little Rock Nine received the Congressional Gold Medal. They also received personal invitations to Barack Obama's inauguration in 2009.

The Little Rock desegregation crisis was one of the first tests of *Brown v. Board of Education*. Though desegregation remained a political issue throughout the civil rights movement, the nature of American education had been forever changed by the courageous actions of the Little Rock Nine.

Carlotta Walls LaNier displays the Congressional Medal of Honor that she and the other members of the Little Rock Nine were awarded by President Bill Clinton in 1999.

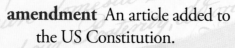

amendment An article added to the US Constitution.

barricade A barrier or roadblock to keep people and vehicles from getting through.

bayonet A knife blade that can be attached to the muzzle of a gun for hand to hand fighting.

civil rights The rights of a citizen, especially to have political and social freedom and equality.

comply To do what is asked in an agreement or command.

correspondence To convey information by letters or emails instead of in person.

desegregation When a policy of racial segregation is ended.

harass To bother, annoy, or torment someone constantly and repeatedly.

incite To encourage or stir up violent or destructive behavior.

injunction A court order that either forces someone to do something or prevents them from doing it.

integrate To mix a minority group of people with a majority group, especially when they were previously separated by race.

jeer To mock or make fun of.

occupied To have taken possession or control of buildings or public spaces.

progressive Having to do with social reform and new ideas.

recruit To enroll or enlist someone in a group or organization.

screening To evaluate or test someone to see if they have certain characteristics or qualities.

segregation The forced separation of different racial groups in a community, country, or place of business.

tactic An action or strategy carefully planned to meet a specific goal.

taunt To provoke or challenge someone by insulting them.

unsheathe To remove a blade from a sheath or scabbard and hold it in a menacing way.

American Civil Liberties Union (ACLU)
125 Broad Street, 18th Floor
New York, NY 10004
(212) 549-2500
Website: https://www.aclu.org
Facebook: @aclu.nationwide
Twitter: @ACLU
Instagram: @aclu_nationwide
The ACLU works to defend and preserve the individual rights and lib-
    erties guaranteed by the constitution and laws of the United States.

Canadian Civil Liberties Association (CCLA)
90 Eglinton Avenue E, Suite 900
Toronto, ON M4P 1A6
Canada
(416) 363-0321
Website: https://ccla.org
Facebook: @BCCivLib
Twitter: @cancivlib
Instagram: @civlib
CCLA fights for the civil liberties, human rights, and democratic free-
    doms of all people across Canada.

Congress of Racial Equality (CORE)
730 West Cheyenne Avenue, Suite 150
North Las Vegas, NV 89030
(702) 637-7968
Website: http://www.congressofracialequality.org

Facebook: https://www.facebook.com/CORE-Immigration-Support
-212477068813300
Twitter: @COREcivilrights
CORE is one of America's original civil rights groups. Founded in 1942, it fights for the rights and interests of minorities and the impoverished.

National Association for the Advancement of Colored People (NAACP)
4805 Mount Hope Drive
Baltimore, MD 21215
(877) 622-2798
Website: http://www.naacp.org
Facebook: @naacp
Twitter: @NAACP
Instagram: @naacp
The NAACP is dedicated to ensuring the political, educational, social, and economic equality of all persons and eliminating race-based discrimination.

WEBSITES

Because of the changing nature of internet links, Rosen Publishing has developed an online list of websites related to the subject of this book. This site is updated regularly. Please use this link to access this list:

http://www.rosenlinks.com/SCRM/Littlerock

Goodman, Susan E. *The First Step: How One Girl Put Segregation on Trial*. New York, NY: Bloomsbury USA, 2016.

Henningfeld, Diane Andrews. *Little Rock Nine*. Farmington Hills, MI: Greenhaven Press, 2014.

Hooks, Gwendolyn. *If You Were a Kid During the Civil Rights Movement*. New York, NY: Children's Press, 2017.

Jeffrey, Gary. *The Little Rock Nine and the Fight for Equal Education*. New York, NY: Gareth Stevens Publishing, 2012.

Kanefield, Teri. *The Girl from the Tar Paper School: Barbara Rose Johns and the Advent of the Civil Rights Movement*. New York, NY: Harry N. Abrams, 2014.

Krumm, Brian. *The Little Rock Nine: A Primary Source Exploration of the Battle for School Integration*. North Mankato, MN: Capstone Press, 2014.

Lucas, Eileen. *The Little Rock Nine Stand Up for Their Rights*. Minneapolis, MN: Millbrook Press, 2011.

Osborne, Linda Barrett. *Miles to Go for Freedom: Segregation and Civil Rights in the Jim Crow Years*. New York, NY: Harry N. Abrams, 2012.

Tisdale, Rachel. *The Little Rock Nine*. New York, NY: Powerkids Press, 2014.

Tougas, Shelley. *Little Rock Girl 1957: How a Photograph Changed the Fight for Integration*. North Mankato, MN: Compass Point Books, 2011.

Bullard, Sara. *Free At Last: A History of the Civil Rights Movement and Those Who Died in the Struggle*. New York, NY: Oxford University Press, 1994.

"Choices in Little Rock." Facing History and Ourselves, November 2009. https://www.facinghistory.org/sites/default/files/publications/Little _Rock.pdf.

Cosgrove, Ben. "Brave Hearts: Remembering the Little Rock Nine." *Time*, September 23, 2012. http://time.com/3874341/little-rock-nine-1957 -photos/.

DeMillo, Andrew. "School's Integration Legacy Looms Large." *USA Today*, September 22, 2007. http://usatoday30.usatoday.com/news /nation/2007-09-22-littlerock_N.htm.

"Elizabeth Eckford." OneHistory.org. Retrieved April 5, 2017. http:// onehistory.org/Eckford.htm.

Gordon, Noah. "The Little Rock Nine: How Far Has the Country Come?" *The Atlantic*, September 25, 2014. https://www.theatlantic.com /politics/archive/2014/09/the-little-rock-nine/380676/.

History.com staff. "Integration of Central High School." History Channel, 2010. http://www.history.com/topics/black-history /central-high-school-integration.

"The Little Rock Nine: Everyday Heroes of Civil Rights." Kansas City Public Library, November 5, 2009. https://www.kclibrary.org/blog /kc-unbound/little-rock-nine-everyday-heroes-civil-rights.

McBride, Alex. "Supreme Court History: Expanding Civil Rights: Land-mark Cases." PBS, December 2006. http://www.pbs.org/wnet /supremecourt/rights/landmark_brown.html.

Williams, Juan. *Eyes on the Prize: America's Civil Rights Years, 1954–1965*. 30th Anniversary Edition. New York, NY: Penguin Books, 2013.

ABOUT THE AUTHOR

Marcia Amidon Lüsted has written 150 books and over 500 magazine articles for young readers. She is a former editor for Cricket Media and also works in regenerative design and permaculture. She became interested in the civil rights movement after writing some magazine articles about it and has since written several books on civil rights topics, including *Eyewitness to the Tuskegee Airmen*, *African Americans in the Military*, and *The 1964 Civil Rights Act*. Learn more about her books at www .adventuresinnonfiction.com.

PHOTO CREDITS

Cover, pp. 1, 5, 7, 13, 15, 17, 19, 21, 23, 25, 26, 31, 33, 37, 39 Bettmann/Getty Images; pp. 3, 42, 43, 44, 45, 46, 47 Onur Ersin /Shutterstock.com; pp. 4, 6, 8, 10, 12, 14, 16, 18, 20, 22, 24, 28, 30, 32, 34, 36, 38, back cover Sergey Kamshylin/Shutterstock.com; p. 9 Thomas D. McAvoy/The LIFE Picture Collection/Getty Images; p. 11 Francis Miller/The LIFE Picture Collection/Getty Images; p. 29 Grey Villet/The LIFE Picture Collection/Getty Images; p. 35 FPG/Archive Photos/Getty Images; p. 41 Kathryn Scott Osler/Denver Post/Getty Images.

Designer: Nelson Sá; Editor and Photo Researcher: Xina M. Uhl